W 75

1/40

J
954
1

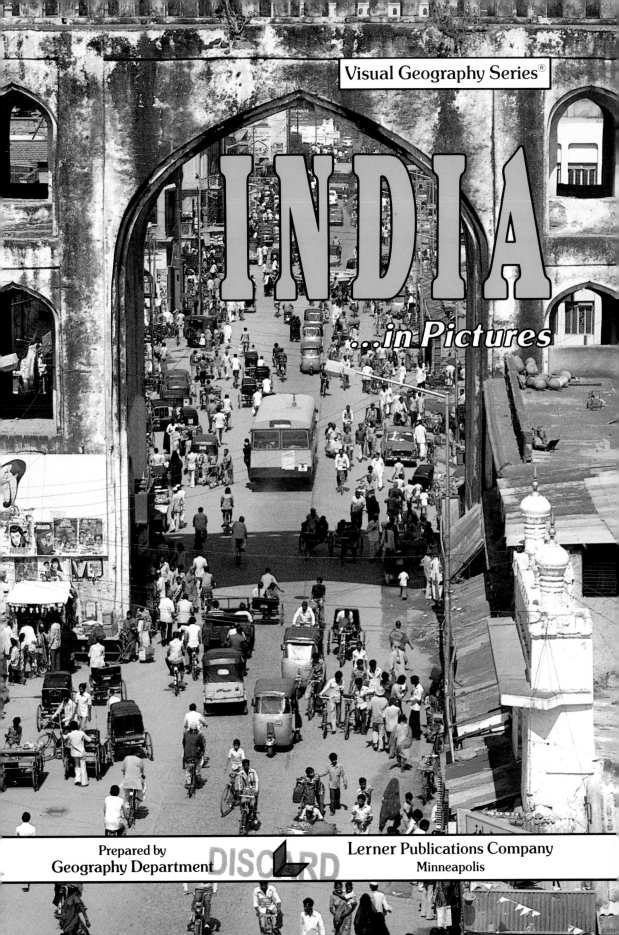

Visual Geography Series®

INDIA

...in Pictures

Prepared by
Geography Department

Lerner Publications Company
Minneapolis

DISCARD

Independent Picture Service

**A woman in the state of Andhra Pradesh prepares her
family's daily meal.**

This is an all-new edition of the Visual Geography
Series. Previous editions have been published by
Sterling Publishing Company, New York City, and
some of the original textual information has been retained. New photographs, maps, charts, captions, and
updated information have been added. The text has
been entirely reset in 10/12 Century Textbook.

LIBRARY OF CONGRESS CATALOGING-IN-PUBLICATION DATA

India in pictures / prepared by Geography Department.
   p. cm. — (Visual geography series)
   Includes index.
   Summary: Photographs and text introduce the
geography, history, government, society, and economy of this diverse nation.
   ISBN 0-8225-1852-X
   1. India. [1. India.] I. Lerner Publications Company. Geography Dept. II. Series: Visual geography
series (Minneapolis, Minn.)
DS407.I447 1989
954—dc19   88-9018
                           CIP
                           AC

International Standard Book Number: 0-8225-1852-X
Library of Congress Catalog Card Number: 88-9018

VISUAL GEOGRAPHY SERIES®

Publisher
Harry Jonas Lerner
Associate Publisher
Nancy M. Campbell
Senior Editor
Mary M. Rodgers
Editor
Gretchen Bratvold
Assistant Editors
Dan Filbin
Kathleen S. Heidel
Illustrations Editor
Karen A. Sirvaitis
Consultants/Contributors
Nathan Rabe
Sandra K. Davis
Designer
Jim Simondet
Cartographer
Carol F. Barrett
Indexer
Sylvia Timian
Production Manager
Gary J. Hansen

Courtesy of Nathan Rabe

**In Agra, India, a visitor contemplates the architecture of
the tomb of the Mughal emperor Akbar.**

Acknowledgments

Title page photo courtesy of Nathan Rabe.

Elevation contours adapted from *The Times Atlas of
the World*, seventh comprehensive edition (New York:
Times Books, 1985).

2 3 4 5 6 7 8 9 10 98 97 96 95 94 93 92 91 90 89

Young Indians play on a sandy beach in the former French enclave (foreign territory) of Pondicherry on India's Coromandel Coast.

Contents

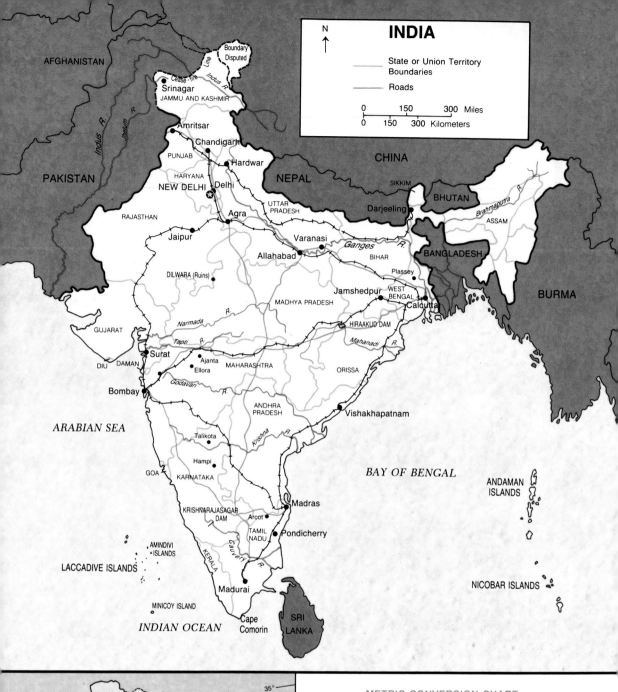

N

INDIA

State or Union Territory
Boundaries

Roads

| 0 | 150 | 300 Miles |
| 0 | 150 | 300 Kilometers |

AFGHANISTAN

Boundary
Disputed

Cease-fire Line

Indus R.

Srinagar
JAMMU AND KASHMIR

CHINA

Amritsar
Chandigarh
Hardwar
PUNJAB
HARYANA
NEW DELHI · Delhi

NEPAL

SIKKIM

BHUTAN

Darjeeling
ASSAM
Brahmaputra R.

PAKISTAN

Indus R.
Jhelum R.

RAJASTHAN

Jaipur

Agra

UTTAR
PRADESH

Varanasi
Allahabad
Ganges
BIHAR
Plassey

WEST
BENGAL
Calcutta

BANGLADESH

BURMA

DILWARA (Ruins)

MADHYA PRADESH

Jamshedpur

HIRAAKUD DAM

Mahanadi R.

GUJARAT

Narmada

Tapti R.

Surat

Ajanta
Ellora

MAHARASHTRA

ORISSA

DIU
DAMAN

Godavari R.

ARABIAN SEA

Bombay

Talikota

ANDHRA
PRADESH

Vishakhapatnam

Krishna R.

Hampi

GOA

KARNATAKA

BAY OF BENGAL

ANDAMAN
ISLANDS

KRISHNARAJASAGAR
DAM

Arcot

Madras

Pondicherry

TAMIL
NADU

AMINDIVI
ISLANDS

Cauvery R.

KERALA

LACCADIVE ISLANDS

NICOBAR ISLANDS

Madurai

MINICOY ISLAND

Cape
Comorin

SRI
LANKA

INDIAN OCEAN

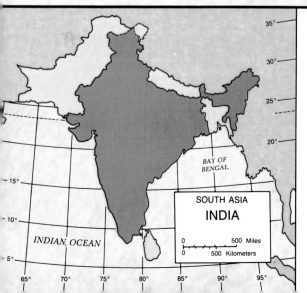

35°

30°

25°

20°

BAY OF
BENGAL

15°

10°

INDIAN OCEAN

5°

65° 70° 75° 80° 85° 90° 95°

SOUTH ASIA
INDIA

| 0 | 500 Miles |
| 0 | 500 Kilometers |

METRIC CONVERSION CHART
To Find Approximate Equivalents

WHEN YOU KNOW:	MULTIPLY BY:	TO FIND:
AREA		
acres	0.41	hectares
square miles	2.59	square kilometers
CAPACITY		
gallons	3.79	liters
LENGTH		
feet	30.48	centimeters
yards	0.91	meters
miles	1.61	kilometers
MASS (weight)		
pounds	0.45	kilograms
tons	0.91	metric tons
VOLUME		
cubic yards	0.77	cubic meters
TEMPERATURE		
degrees Fahrenheit	0.56 (*after* subtracting 32)	degrees Celsius

The Mughals unified nearly all of India between the sixteenth and eighteenth centuries. This tomb houses the remains of the early Mughal emperor Humayun and features tall, arched entrances and a domed roof.

Introduction

Covering a vast peninsula in southern Asia known as the Indian subcontinent, India is a nation of both diversity and division. Until it gained independence from Great Britain in 1947, India only rarely experienced national unity. Even during periods of cohesion, however, large areas within the country remained beyond the complete control of any central government. Before formal unification, India comprised hundreds of separate kingdoms and princedoms. Because of this varied history, India sometimes appears to be not just one nation, but many.

In present-day India, most household technology is basic, and modern services —such as clean water and electricity— have not become universal. Yet India has a thriving and varied economy, in which almost all products are made within the country using Indian equipment. Indian satellites orbit the earth, an Indian astronaut has flown in space, and computers are common in the Indian workplace.

As the world's most populous democracy, India has a strong voice in Asian affairs. Elections are held regularly, and writers debate the issues in one of Asia's freest presses—with over 20,000 journals and newspapers that express a wide range of viewpoints.

Despite these signs of growth and progress, India faces many difficulties. Internal violence, particularly in the state of Punjab in northwestern India, mars the unity of the country. In addition, at least 40 percent of the population live in poverty. With its long and eventful history, India endeavors to secure its footing in the world community and to develop Indian answers to the challenges of the twenty-first century.

The Himalaya Mountains stretch from Pakistan to eastern India and include many peaks that are over 20,000 feet in height. Snow-covered throughout the year, the range overlooks forested valleys and rugged terrain.

Courtesy of Nathan Rabe

1) The Land

Millions of years ago, two sections of the huge landmass called Gondwanaland collided, causing a great buckling movement to occur. This event created the Himalaya Mountains and forced the earth's crust to fold downward, forming a wide trench that has been filling with sand, mud, and stones ever since. Two of India's four main regions—the Himalayas and the Indo-Gangetic Plain—exist as a result of this early geologic event.

India and Pakistan both occupy parts of the Indian subcontinent, which the two countries agreed to share under the partition arrangement of 1947. India's portion of the subcontinent covers almost 1.2 million square miles, making India the seventh largest country in the world. Its area equals about two-fifths of the continental United States. India's maximum length from north to south is 2,000 miles. Its maximum width is 1,700 miles from west to east.

Included in India's national territory are several small groups of islands. The Andaman and Nicobar island chains are scattered over nearly 500 miles in the Bay of Bengal, and the Laccadive, Minicoy, and Amindivi islands lie to the west, off the Malabar Coast.

India is bounded on the northwest and north by Pakistan, China, Nepal, and Bhutan, and on the east by Burma. Bangladesh (formerly East Pakistan) cuts between the Indian states of West Bengal and Assam. India's southeastern shoreline is called the Coromandel Coast, and its southwestern limit is known as the Malabar Coast.

Most of India is a peninsula surrounded by three large bodies of water—the Arabian Sea to the west, the Indian Ocean to the south, and the Bay of Bengal to the east. The island nation of Sri Lanka lies 40 miles southeast of India in the Bay of Bengal.

Topography

India's terrain varies a great deal but is made up of four general areas. In the extreme north is a section of the Himalaya Mountains. South of the Himalayas and their foothills lies the vast, generally level Indo-Gangetic Plain, which extends into Pakistan, Nepal, and Bangladesh. In the central section of peninsular, or southern, India lies the Deccan Plateau, which is surrounded by three low mountain ranges. These mountains compose the fourth region and consist of the Eastern Ghats, the Western Ghats, and the Vindhya Mountains to the north.

HIMALAYAS

The tallest mountain range in the world, the Himalayas block India from the rest of central Asia. The entire range extends for 1,500 miles in an arc from northern to northeastern India and contains many high peaks. Within India, the highest is

Photo by Bernice K. Condit

At Cape Comorin—India's southernmost point—the waters of the Bay of Bengal, the Indian Ocean, and the Arabian Sea meet.

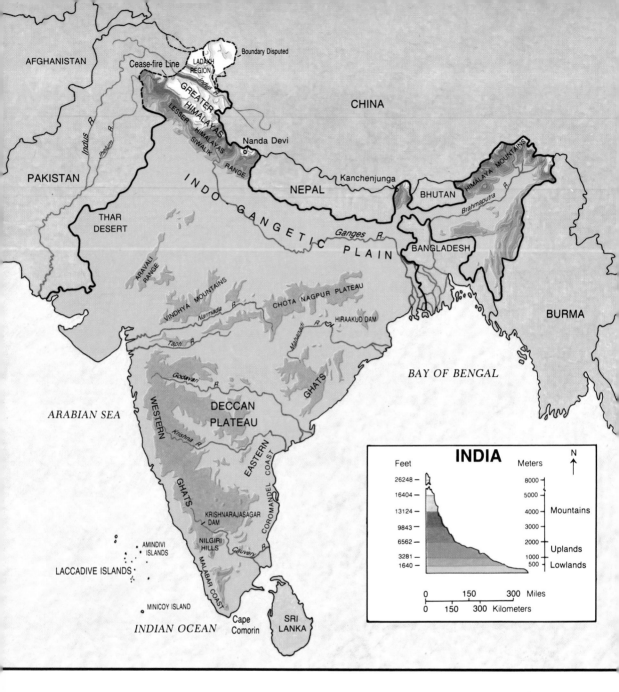

Kanchenjunga (28,146 feet), which lies on the nation's border with Nepal.

Geologists note several subregions within the Himalayas and believe that movements of both the subcontinent and central Asia still occur. Subregions in India include the Siwalik Range that lies in the Himalayan foothills, the Lesser Himalayas that rise to heights of about 10,000 feet above sea level, and the Greater Himalayas that contain India's highest peaks.

INDO-GANGETIC PLAIN

The Indo-Gangetic Plain is named for the two great rivers—the Indus and the Ganges—that border it on the west and east. Most of this 200-mile-wide plain consists of flat, well-watered land.

Since its formation millions of years ago, the northern plain has collected thousands of tons of fertile earth that rivers have carried from the mountains. In addition to bringing deposits of excellent topsoil, India's rivers regularly water the plain.

Despite being well-watered, the western section of the Indo-Gangetic Plain merges into the Thar Desert, which is located between the Aravali Range and the Indus River. Within India, the Thar Desert stretches into the states of Rajasthan and Gujarat.

DECCAN PLATEAU

Southern India, made up mostly of the Deccan Plateau, is a single plate of land. As a result, the Deccan has been geologically stable for a long stretch of time, unlike the Himalayas and the Indo-Gangetic Plain, which were formed more recently from continental movement.

Courtesy of UNICEF

In India's flat regions, such as the Indo-Gangetic Plain, waterways that originate in the Himalayas flow through the land providing recreation as well as irrigation.

Courtesy of Air-India Library

A river travels among the tea-covered Nilgiri Hills in the state of Tamil Nadu, bringing fertility to the surrounding farmland.

The triangular Deccan Plateau begins south of the Narmada River and comes to a point at Cape Comorin in the southern state of Tamil Nadu. Averaging between 1,000 and 2,300 feet above sea level, the plateau includes sections of rolling hills through which many rivers flow.

SOUTHERN MOUNTAIN RANGES

Surrounding the Deccan Plateau on three sides are low mountain ranges. To the north, the Vindhya Mountains separate the plateau from the Indo-Gangetic Plain. The range's highest peak is 3,651 feet above sea level, and the entire chain runs parallel to the Narmada River.

Boats and the branches of coconut trees crowd a waterway in the state of Kerala along India's Malabar Coast.

A coastal strip separates the Eastern Ghats from the Bay of Bengal. This 500-mile-long range averages 1,500 to 2,000 feet in height and extends as far north as the Mahanadi River. Another coastal belt divides the Western Ghats from the Arabian Sea. These mountains stretch for 800 miles along the western coast and reach heights of 3,000 to 5,000 feet. Their northernmost point lies at the mouth of the Tapti River. The two ranges merge in southern India at the Nilgiri Hills in Tamil Nadu.

Rivers

India has several long rivers, which are flanked on either side by stretches of fertile soil. Northern waterways receive the melting snows of the Himalayas. Many rivers, including the Krishna, drain into the Bay of Bengal. The principal waterways in northern India are the Ganges, with its many tributaries, and the Indus.

Faithful Hindus, who regard the waters of the Ganges River as sacred, gather at the river's edge in the city of Varanasi to bathe, to exercise, and to perform religious rites.

10

Although polluted, the 1,500-mile-long Ganges is still important for agricultural irrigation. The Ganges begins in the Himalayas and flows south into the Indo-Gangetic Plain at Hardwar. Eventually, the river travels east to join the Brahmaputra, and together they empty into the Bay of Bengal at Calcutta. Hindus regard the Ganges as sacred and, despite the health hazards, drink and bathe in its waters. The sacred Hindu cities of Allahabad and Varanasi are located along the river's banks.

The Indus originates in southern China and flows mostly through Pakistan. A small section of the river also lies within Jammu and Kashmir—a territory whose ownership is claimed by both India and Pakistan. One reason why the two countries are fighting over Jammu and Kashmir is that the nation controlling the state will also control the Indus River. By diverting the river, India could deprive Pakistan of water for irrigation.

Photo by K. J. Chugh, Dinodia Picture Agency

An upper section of the Indus River makes its way through Ladakh in the disputed territory of Jammu and Kashmir. Under the terms of the 1949 cease-fire agreement, India was assigned the southern part of Ladakh, and Pakistan got the northern area.

Photo by Bernice K. Condit

Hindus consider the Godavari River to be one of the holiest waterways on the Deccan Plateau. The river travels through the city of Nasik in the state of Maharashtra, affording these women a place to wash their clothes.

Boats crowd the Jhelum River, which flows through the city of Srinagar— the capital of Jammu and Kashmir— and which eventually joins the Indus.

Rivers crisscross the Deccan Plateau, providing it with water for both crops and hydroelectric power. The Mahanadi rises in the Vindhya Mountains and eventually flows through the state of Orissa. Because of its large water volume in the flood season, the river has become important for irrigation, and the Hiraakud hydroelectric plant is powered by its flow. In addition, the river basin is an important rice-growing region.

Farther south, the Godavari begins near the city of Bombay and wends its way toward the Bay of Bengal, where it empties through several mouths. The Cauvery reaches the Bay of Bengal through a wide delta and provides irrigation for the surrounding southern regions. Hindus also regard the waters of the Cauvery as sacred.

Climate

India has a reputation for being hot and dry, but the nation is so large that it contains a wide range of climates. For example, the northern third of India—which includes the Himalayas—experiences seasonal temperatures and cool winters. The rest of the country has temperatures that change from warm to hot throughout the year, with April and May being the hottest months. In the inland areas, the temperature sometimes rises to 120° F during those months, and it can reach 105° F on the Indo-Gangetic Plain. In the south, summer temperatures remain at about 100° F.

Humidity and rainfall levels also vary throughout India. The rainy season occurs from mid-June to mid-September, when moisture-bearing winds arrive from the Arabian Sea and the Bay of Bengal. These seasonal winds, called monsoons, are responsible for India's distinct rainy and dry periods. During the summer, the southwest monsoon travels northward from the Indian Ocean, and the northeast monsoon arrives in winter from Siberia. This second monsoon brings extremely dry weather and, at times, severe storms.

The Malabar Coast and West Bengal receive the heaviest rainfall—over 100 inches annually—and have the most humid weather. The eastern half of the Indo-Gangetic Plain is also rainy and receives 40 to 80 inches annually. Most of the Deccan Plateau has moderate precipitation— 20 to 40 inches per year—and the arid Thar Desert gets less than 10 inches of annual rainfall.

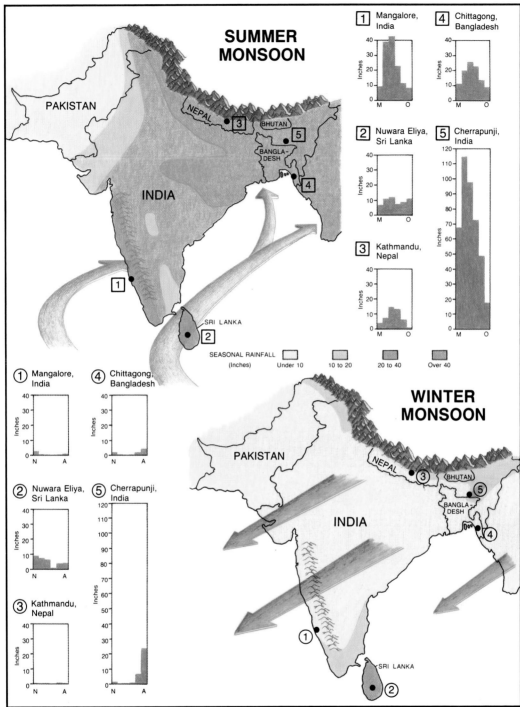

Artwork by Carol F. Barrett

These maps show the seasonal shift of winds, called monsoons, over southern Asia and the rainfall levels for five cities in the region. In summer (May to October), the monsoon winds blow from sea to land, carrying moisture—which is released as rain—as they pass over this part of the Asian continent. In winter (November to April), the monsoons blow from land to sea. Because they originate over a cold, arid land surface, the winter winds are dry, and little or no rainfall is associated with them. Mangalore, India, on the edge of the Western Ghats mountains, gets generous rains as the summer monsoon winds rise up over the low mountains. On the other hand, Cherrapunji—which is located at the base of the eastern Himalayas—receives enormous amounts of summer rain (115 inches in June alone). The Himalayas force the winds to rise sharply, causing the air to cool quickly and to dump its moisture on the land below. Climate data taken from *World-Climates* by Willy Rudloff, Stuttgart, 1981.

Flora and Fauna

Despite heavy rainfall and fertile soil, only about one-quarter of India is forested, and much of this woodland supports scrub vegetation. Where rainfall is heavy—in the Western Ghats and in the state of Assam, for example—tropical rain-forests thrive and feature dense stands of evergreen, bamboo, and teak trees. The moist regions give way to swampy lowlands that include mangrove thickets. Drier tropical cover emerges in areas with less than 100 inches of annual rainfall, and clusters of sal and teak trees are common.

India also has hot, dry regions, where the natural vegetation must be drought-resistant to survive. Bushes and thorny plants, including members of the *Capparis* and *Zizyphus* families, compose most of the sparse plant life in arid areas. The low temperatures of the Himalayas, on the other hand, demand plant life that can withstand cold conditions. Cedar and pine grow well in the northwestern section of the mountains, and rhododendron trees and shrubs also survive.

To feed its growing population, India has turned much of its grassland and for-

En route to the northeastern city of Darjeeling in West Bengal, the hillsides are covered with vegetation.

Courtesy of Jeannine Bayard and Kip Lilly

Smaller-eared than their African cousins, Indian elephants can grow to heights of 10 feet and can weigh over 10,000 pounds. Herds are usually made up of mature females, young elephants of both sexes, and one older male elephant.

Courtesy of Air-India Library

Bengal tigers are found in central and southern India, as well as on the Southeast Asian mainland. The animals are solitary and usually live in grassy areas or forests, where they prey on deer, cattle, and other animals.

ests into farmland. As a result, animal habitats are becoming scarce, and the number of large mammals is dwindling. Only a few gaur—the largest wild oxen in the world—survive in India, and both the rhinoceros and the lion are nearing extinction on the subcontinent. Fewer than 2,000 Indian tigers remain, but smaller cats, such as the snow leopard, are still fairly common. Asiatic elephants, whose main habitats are in the remote forests of the Deccan Plateau and in the northeastern Himalayas, continue to be used as work animals in densely wooded areas.

More than 2,000 kinds of birds live on the subcontinent, and reptile species are also numerous. Three varieties of crocodiles inhabit India's rivers, and the mahseer is the most prized freshwater fish.

Cities

India has nearly 100 cities with populations that exceed 100,000; several urban areas have populations of more than one million. Yet only 15 percent of the nation's inhabitants live in cities.

Overshadowed by the high-rise buildings of Bombay, low-income Indians pick through rubble and garbage to find items to repair and sell.

A crowded market in Calcutta suggests the high population density that exists in this city in the state of West Bengal. Estimates indicate that 79,000 people live within every square mile of the city's territory.

Bombay, India's largest city and main port on the western coast, has a total metropolitan population of 10 million. The city is actually an island that is linked to the mainland by many bridges. Wealthy residents of Bombay live in modern apartments in the city's older sections, which also contain historical and commercial landmarks from its early history as a British trading center. Cheap and poorly serviced housing developments surround Bombay, and overcrowding has resulted in makeshift dwellings and thousands of homeless Indians.

Lying in northeastern India along the Bay of Bengal, Calcutta is India's second largest city, with 9.1 million people in its metropolitan area. In addition to being the chief port for India's trade with Southeast Asia, Calcutta also has some of the world's worst cases of overcrowding, poverty, and neglect. Religious and political riots have erupted in Calcutta on several occasions in the last few decades. Nevertheless, the

Ships stand at dockside in Calcutta, which—despite its long-standing problems of unemployment and overpopulation— remains a major port on the Bay of Bengal.

The Jami Masjid—the largest Islamic place of worship, or mosque, in India—overlooks Delhi, which was the capital city under both the Mughals and the British. Distinct from New Delhi (India's modern capital), Delhi displays architectural styles from many eras of India's history.

city has retained its position as the shipping outlet for locally produced jute (a fiber used in rope making) and minerals.

Delhi, the capital of India from 1912 to 1931, has a metropolitan population of 5.7 million. Thousands of Indian refugees arrived in Delhi from newly formed Pakistan after the division of the Indian subcontinent into Hindu and Muslim states in 1947. This migration has contributed to a fourfold population increase since 1951. New Delhi (population 370,000)—with which old Delhi is sometimes combined—is located just south of Delhi and became India's capital in 1931. The slums and narrow streets of the crowded old city contrast sharply with the wide thoroughfares and modern buildings of New Delhi. An important railway hub in northwestern India, Delhi also produces manufactured goods.

Located in the state of Tamil Nadu, Madras (population 4.2 million) has developed from a small village into a chief port on India's southeastern coast. Britain planned the city's growth during colonial times because it wanted a safe port on the Bay of Bengal. Madras contains many industrial plants, such as auto assembly facilities, cotton mills, and leather tanneries. Cement, glass, and iron factories also bring prosperity to the region.

Mohenjo-Daro was one of the main cities of the Indus civilization, which flourished in western India and eastern Pakistan between 2500 B.C. and 1800 B.C. British archaeologists discovered the ruins of the city in 1922, and so far experts have excavated about 250 acres of the ancient urban center.

2) History and Government

India did not develop as one nation in a continuous series of events. Rather, many kingdoms and conquerors occupied various parts of the subcontinent. The earliest history generally takes place in northern India, although some powerful realms eventually stretched southward.

Archaeological evidence has revealed early communities of humans in India about 4000 B.C. These people were hunters and gatherers who lived in permanent villages.

The Indus Civilization

Scientists believe that large-scale settlement of the Indian subcontinent occurred about 2500 B.C. along the fertile banks of the Indus River and its many tributaries. A complex urban civilization grew in this region, which at its peak included what are now Pakistan and western India. Archaeologists have uncovered over 300 well-designed cities that featured unique architectural styles and languages. The two main urban centers were Mohenjo-Daro and Harappa, both located in eastern Pakistan.

The Indus civilization standardized weights and measures and produced surplus crops to trade. Its cities had extensive drainage systems, well-defined neighborhoods, and fortified administrative headquarters. A system of picture writing

Among the many figures uncovered from the ruins at Mohenjo-Daro are a sculpted animal head *(above)* and a figure of a king or priest *(right)*.

existed but has yet to be deciphered by modern experts. Either environmental factors—such as flooding or overpopulation—or invasion caused the Indus civilization to decline about 1800 B.C.

The Aryans

Arriving from south central Asia between 2000 and 1000 B.C., a group of people called Aryans conquered and ruled the Ganges region of India. To escape Aryan

The Indus pictographic system of writing—as yet undeciphered by language experts—appears on a clay seal above the figure of a bull.

power, most of the local inhabitants—who have come to be called Dravidians—moved south into peninsular India.

The Aryans developed a philosophical and social system that evolved into Hinduism, a religion that involved the worship of several gods. The highly structured framework included a caste system, under which citizens became members of rigid social and professional groups. In addition to spreading their philosophy, the Aryans brought iron tools, the horse and chariot, and knowledge of astronomy and mathematics to the region.

Sixteen separate states arose in the Aryan territory during the next 1,000 years. The realms stretched across the northern plain from modern Afghanistan to Bangladesh and were closely tied to the Hindu religion, whose priests supported the authority of rulers and helped to enforce the caste system.

By about the middle of the sixth century B.C., the Magadha kingdom had emerged as the dominant Aryan state. Its rise was accompanied by religious reform movements that resulted in the founding of Buddhism and Jainism, both religious offshoots of Hinduism. Magadha's location in northeastern India at the crossroads of major trade routes, as well as its access to rich soil and iron deposits, helped to establish its stability.

The Maurya Dynasty

In 326 B.C., during the reign of the Magadha ruler Candragupta Maurya, Alexander the Great of Greece conquered the northwestern region of India. Alexander's death in 323 B.C. hindered the spread of Greek influence, but the generals he left behind to govern territories in Bactria and Sogdiana (now in Afghanistan and the Soviet Union) produced some links between the Indian and Greek cultures.

Candragupta founded the Maurya dynasty (family of rulers), which governed nearly all of India for about a century.

In the west central state of Maharashtra, many religious temples (often called caves) have been uncovered. Hewn from solid rock, these religious sites date from about 100 B.C. to roughly A.D. 1000. This image of Gautama Buddha—the founder of the Buddhist religion—was carved about 2,200 years ago in the Ajanta caves.

The Ellora caves are slightly younger than those at Ajanta and are a mixture of Buddhist, Hindu, and Jain religious structures. This ornate pillar dating from about A.D. 700 decorates the entrance of a Buddhist vihara, or monastery.

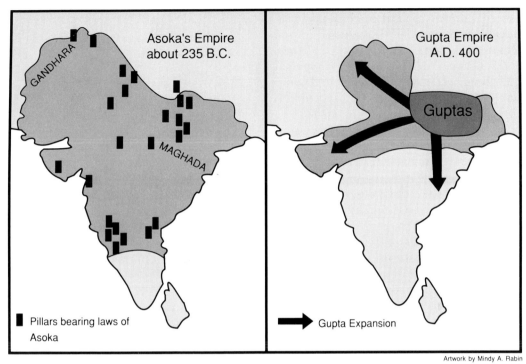

The empire *(left)* of the Maurya ruler Asoka stretched from present-day Afghanistan to eastern India and went as far south as the modern states of Karnataka and Andhra Pradesh. By about A.D. 400 the Gupta Empire *(right)* covered the northern third of the Indian subcontinent.

The most famous of the Maurya rulers was Candragupta's grandson Asoka, who reigned from 273 to 232 B.C. He made Buddhism the official religion of India and encouraged the construction of many massive Buddhist buildings.

Buddhism's philosophy of nonviolence inspired Asoka to renounce force as a means of governing. His laws, which were carved on huge pillars, focused on social duty and included themes of tolerance and harmony. These ideas worked well within Asoka's large, diverse realm, but the emperor—not his principles—had become the guiding force of the empire. Within a century of Asoka's death in 232 B.C., the empire shrank back within the borders of Magadha, and no lasting regional powers arose in the north for several centuries. Nevertheless, trade routes between India and the Persian, Chinese, and Roman empires developed.

Guptas, Ephthalites, and Rajputs

The separate kingdoms that followed the death of Asoka came together in the fourth and fifth centuries A.D. under a new Hindu dynasty, the Guptas. The period of Gupta rule is called the golden age of India, because it fostered discoveries in mathematics, astronomy, and the arts. Scholars compiled Sanskrit—the language of the wealthy—into dictionaries, and mathematicians calculated the shape and movement of the planets.

During the golden age, social pressures encouraged women to marry early. Gupta governments approved of suttee—burning a widow with the body of her husband when he died. The caste system preserved strong social divisions, and slavery was widely practiced.

The Ephthalites, a fierce central Asian people, invaded the region in the second half of the fifth century and weakened the

Artwork by Mindy A. Rabin

Gupta Empire. By the seventh century, dynasties throughout northern India were competing for territory. Many of these rivals belonged to the Rajput clan, which had a reputation for being aggressive and warlike.

Rajput rulers protected their lands from outsiders but did little to develop them internally. As a result, commerce declined and farming remained traditional. Their isolation also made the Rajputs unaware of outside events. One of these events was the rise of Islam, a monotheistic (one-god) religion founded in the seventh century by the prophet Muhammad in what is now Saudi Arabia. The new faith urged believers to expand their territory and to convert conquered peoples to Islam.

Muslim Rule

Control of India by followers of the Islamic religion, who were called Muslims, came through a series of military and cultural conquests over five centuries. The Muslims arrived in India soon after the death of Muhammad in A.D. 632. Waves of newly converted Arab traders followed, and these merchants brought their faith with them as they conducted business on India's western coast.

Muslim military attacks on northern India began in earnest under Mahmud of Ghazna, who ruled Khorasan (a region in what is now northeastern Iran) from 999 to 1030. In A.D. 1000 Mahmud launched the first of over 15 military invasions into India. The disunited Indians of the north-

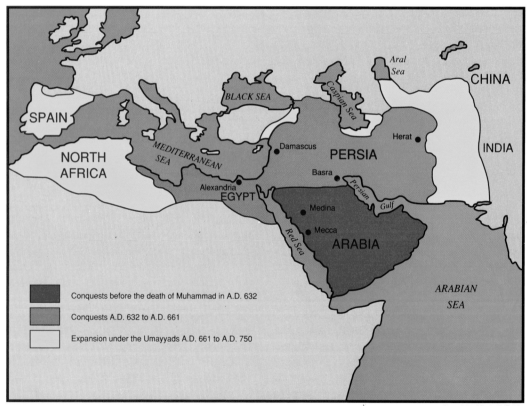

Artwork by Mindy A. Rabin

Beginning in the late seventh century A.D., armies made up of Muslims—followers of the Islamic religion—invaded India, as well as regions that are now part of Pakistan and Afghanistan. In their wake came Arab merchants, who established commercial links along India's coasts. It was not until the eleventh century, however, that Muslim conquerors were able to take full control of the subcontinent.

Qutb-ud-Din Aybak, an early ruler of the Delhi sultanate (kingdom), began this 240-foot-high tower as a victory monument. It commemorated the defeat of the last Hindu kingdom in Delhi. Now called the Qutb Minar, the tower is a good example of early Islamic architecture.

ern plain were unable to resist the attacks, and by 1025 Mahmud had added the Punjab region to his empire.

Muhammad Ghuri completed the Muslim conquest of India in 1193. He established his capital at Delhi and went on to subdue northern India as far east as Bengal. Five dynasties of the Delhi sultanate (kingdom) ruled during the period of Muslim control in India, and each came to power by violence.

Muhammad Ghuri's successor, a former slave named Qutb-ud-Din Aybak, was the first ruler of the Slave dynasty, which lasted from 1206 to 1290. The succeeding dynasties of the Delhi sultanate—the Khalji, the Tughluq, the Sayyid, and the Lodi—consolidated their control over northern India between 1260 and 1526.

During the 320-year period of the Delhi sultanate, clashes often occurred between Muslims and subject Hindu populations. Occasionally, the two cultures blended successfully. At other times, Muslim religious intolerance brought about the destruction of Hindu temples and resulted in distrust between the two groups.

The Delhi sultanate slowly declined after 1398, when the Mongol conqueror Timur the Lame (also known as Tamerlane) swept down from central Asia and sacked Delhi. The Delhi sultanate survived for only one more century before falling in 1526 to Zahir-ud-Din Muhammad, a descendant of Timur.

The Development of Kingdoms in Southern India

In the south, on the Deccan Plateau, a large, strong state formed in the third century B.C. under the rule of the Andhra (or Satavahana) dynasty. The 30 successive Andhra kings, who reigned over a period of four centuries (from 230 B.C. to about A.D. 230), made up the longest continuous dynasty ever to rule in India. In their flourishing kingdom, Buddhism existed alongside Hinduism. The Andhra kings raided the north but never gained lasting control of any part of it, and, after Andhra collapsed in the third century A.D., southern India became a mosaic of small realms.

The southernmost part of present-day India experienced centuries of conflict among three Dravidian kingdoms. The three dynasties—the Cola, the Chera, and the Pandya—had cultural connections with

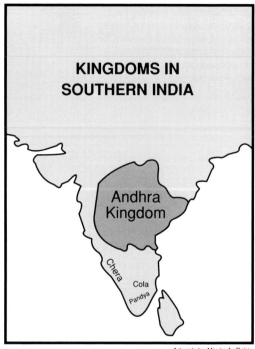

KINGDOMS IN SOUTHERN INDIA

Artwork by Mindy A. Rabin

In the southern regions of the subcontinent, the Andhra dynasty (family of rulers) emerged in about the third century B.C. Several centuries later, the Cola, Pandya, and Chera dynasties competed for control of southernmost India.

Photo by Ruthi Soudack

A fifteenth-century frieze (carved band) on the Vittala Temple was sculpted during the Vijayanagar period. The artwork depicts dancers, military outfits, and forms of transport used near modern Hampi—the site of the capital of the Vijayanagar Empire.

The extensive ruins of Golconda Fort lie near the city of Hyderabad. The stronghold was built by the Qutb Shahi family, who governed one of the five subdivisions of the Bahmani kingdom in the sixteenth century.

kingdoms to the north but maintained their independence.

The Colas eventually emerged as the strongest group and expanded their holdings to include the islands of Sri Lanka and Maldives in the tenth and eleventh centuries A.D. The Cola navy became the strongest military force in the southern region and helped to found an empire that lasted through the thirteenth century.

Conflicts in the South

The Cola dynasty gave way to that of the Vijayanagars, a Hindu people from the modern state of Karnataka. Founded in 1336, the dynasty depended on its commercial contacts, trading centers, and network of roads for its economic and political survival.

In 1347 a rival realm, the Bahmani kingdom, emerged in the south as an offshoot of the Muslim Delhi sultanate. Eventual-

ly, the Bahmani kingdom subdivided into five Muslim states. Efforts by the Bahmani kingdom to expand its holdings led to frequent conflicts with the Vijayanagar Empire.

In 1565 the five Muslim states joined together to defeat the Vijayanagars, fighting a final battle at Talikota. Weakened by constant warfare, the kingdoms of the southern peninsula, like those of the northern plain, came under the rule of Mongol invaders from central Asia.

The Mughal Empire

Zahir-ud-Din Muhammad, who was called Babur by his followers, united northern India under his rule between 1526 and 1530 and laid the foundations of the Mughal Empire. (The name Mughal is derived from the word *Mongol.*) The new leaders were talented administrators, military leaders, and diplomats in foreign and domestic

A miniature painting from the period of Mughal rule shows the emperor in conference with his advisers in the royal palace.

affairs. The empire traded heavily and generated immense wealth. Religious tolerance calmed the Hindus, who initially feared the Islamic Mughals would convert them. The realm grew larger through marriage connections or contracts with smaller princedoms, rarely through military conquest. At its height, the Mughal Empire governed nearly all of present-day India.

Although several emperors stand out, the empire reached its peak under Babur's grandson Akbar, who reigned from 1556 to 1605. The emperor sought the goodwill of the Hindus, especially of the Rajputs, and placed some of them in high positions in his government.

Akbar's immediate successors, first Jahangir and then Shah Jahan, were able to hold the empire together with little effort, partly because of the strong organization

that Akbar had left behind. During the reign of Shah Jahan, Indian architecture reached an artistic height that is best illustrated by the Taj Mahal, which the emperor ordered to be built as a mausoleum (above-ground tomb) for his favorite wife.

Shah Jahan's son, Alamgir (also known as Aurangzeb), drove his father from the throne in 1658. A strict Muslim, the new emperor attempted to return to traditional Islamic ways and to expand his empire. As a result, he spent the last 20 years of his reign trying to subdue the Hindu Maratha confederacy in western India and the Deccan states in the south. The Maratha were well-organized fighters and defeated the Mughal armies in most clashes. After the death of Alamgir in 1707, the Mughal Empire began to decline because of constant rebellions.

Built between 1632 and 1653, during the height of the Mughal Empire, the Taj Mahal was the emperor Shah Jahan's monument to his favorite wife, Mumtaz Mahal. The marble structure — decorated with intricate patterns of inlaid precious stones — sits on a raised platform surrounded by four minarets (towers) in Agra, Uttar Pradesh.

The central landmark of the city of Jaipur in the state of Rajasthan is the Palace of the Winds. Constructed in 1799 by Maharaja (prince) Sawaj Pratap Singh, the palace allowed royal women to observe the main street without being seen by ordinary passersby.

The Arrival of the Europeans

Europeans, who had traded with India in ancient times, renewed their contact in 1498, when the Portuguese navigator Vasco da Gama visited the subcontinent. The Portuguese established trade links—at Goa, for example—and brought goods from India to Europe throughout the sixteenth century. Reports of the wealth of Akbar's empire stirred Britain, France, and the Netherlands to compete with Portugal for India's trade.

In the seventeenth century, with the permission of Mughal emperors, the British East India Company established several trading posts in India—at Surat in 1612, at Bombay in 1661, and at Calcutta in 1690. The French also managed to acquire a share of the Indian trade, claiming Pondichéry (now Pondicherry) in 1670. India's relations with Europe were essentially commercial, and both the Mughal emperors and the trading companies profited from the exchange of spices and textiles.

The situation changed suddenly at the beginning of the eighteenth century, when the Mughal Empire began to decline. Re-

Rivalries erupted throughout India at the beginning of the eighteenth century, and Mughal princes on horseback led their armies against competing local princes.

gional rivalries erupted all over India. Fearful of losing their commercial arrangements, Britain and France each made alliances with Indian princes to expel the other European power from India. The Indian princes, in turn, took advantage of the rivalry between the British and the French to gain power over other Indian rulers.

By the mid-eighteenth century India was a chaotic battleground where the British and French fought each other and where Indian princes jockeyed for control. Under the leadership of Robert Clive, British forces defeated the French in 1751 at Arcot (near Madras), and in 1757 they overcame the ruler of Bengal at Plassey, not far from Calcutta.

British Rule

For the next 100 years, Britain steadily extended its influence, and by the middle of the nineteenth century, it had firm control over nearly the entire Indian subcontinent. The expansion and protection of Britain's

Under the command of Robert Clive, British forces defeated Siraj-ud-Dawlah at Plassey in Bengal in 1757. Clive's military efforts helped to found Britain's empire in India.

trade—as well as a desire to secure its territory against both foreign and local threats—motivated the British to become directly involved in Indian affairs. In addition, Britain felt that it should spread European culture—especially Western social ideas and Christianity—throughout its colonial holdings, including India.

Officials of the East India Company exercised political and economic power in India until 1858. Between 1857 and 1858, however, rebellions against British control erupted in Bengal and in central India. Indian nationalists called the conflict the First War of Independence, and the British referred to it as the Sepoy Mutiny.

In May 1857 a group of Sepoys (Indian soldiers in the British army) attacked the imperial capital of Delhi in an effort to reestablish the last Mughal emperor. Although the revolt had many causes, a predominant one was Indian objections to British attempts to convert Hindus and Muslims to Christianity.

After 10 months of fighting, British troops defeated the rebels. As a result of the rebellion, Britain transferred administrative responsibility for India from the East India Company to the British Crown. The British then adopted two policies to ensure that they would have strong control over India and its people. Britain promised not to interfere in the religious affairs of the Indians, and it began to gather the support of Indian leaders and professionals for the British colonial administration.

British India

The term "British India" refers to the region on the subcontinent that was under

At the Kashmir Gate, Sepoys (Indians in the British army) and British soldiers fought for control of Delhi during the Sepoy Mutiny, which lasted from 1857 to 1858.

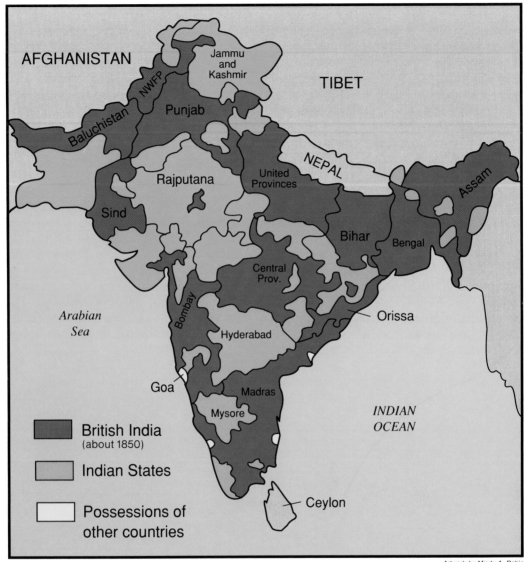

Artwork by Mindy A. Rabin

"British India" was composed of areas directly controlled by the British government. Maharajas had formal authority over the Indian states, and other foreign powers – mainly France and Portugal – retained small land possessions on the coasts.

direct British control. The monarch of Great Britain at the time, Queen Victoria, became empress of India and appointed a series of viceroys to represent her as head of the Indian government. A resident official of the British government indirectly ruled the Indian states—areas where treaties existed between ruling princes and the British—by influencing the local leaders.

The Indian legal system was based on British civil and criminal laws, and some Hindu practices, such as suttee, were outlawed. The British built extensive railway, road, and telegraph networks, widened irrigation systems, and provided food relief during famines.

Britain used India as a source of raw materials and as a market for British-manufactured goods but made little effort to help India remain economically independent. As a result, India's once self-sufficient economy became tied to markets over which it had no control.

Of the changes that came with British rule, discrimination against Indians was among the most far-reaching. Barriers formed that excluded all Indians—even the wealthy and the well educated—from social contact with the British. The Indian army became layered, with only the British serving as officers. These divisions between the British and the Indians helped to stimulate nationalist feelings in India.

Opposition to British Rule

Opposition to British rule emerged slowly, beginning with the formation of the Indian National Congress in 1885. The original aim of the congress was self-rule—but not total independence—for India within the British Empire. For the next several decades, the congress—whose members were mostly Hindus—was the only organization with a national reputation.

British colonial policy encouraged divisions among the people so that no single group could become too powerful. For example, the British supported the creation of the Muslim League in 1906 as a counterbalance to the Indian National Congress.

In 1905 the British viceroy divided Bengal into two separate administrative areas, despite the contrary wishes of local peoples. This move sparked violent reactions and sharpened Indian desires for self-rule. In addition, many Indians objected to the continued economic exploitation of India. Following the disturbances, the British sponsored reform acts, which enlarged the participation of Indians in legislative councils.

Courtesy of Air-India Library

An architectural symbol of British influence on the subcontinent is Calcutta's Victoria Memorial, which was begun in 1906 after the death of Queen Victoria, Britain's monarch and empress of India. Today the structure houses a museum that features artifacts from the colonial period of India's history.

World War I and Its Aftermath

Over one million Indian soldiers fought with British troops in Europe and the Middle East during World War I (1914–1918).

Out of respect for his simple lifestyle and personal philosophy, Mohandas K. Gandhi was given the title Mahatma (Great Soul) by the Indian people. Chosen as president of the Indian National Congress in 1925, he became less formally involved in the resistance movement after resigning the post in 1934. A Hindu extremist assassinated Gandhi in 1948.

Independent Picture Service

India cooperated with Britain partly because it expected that after the war Britain would reward it with self-government.

The Government of India Act of 1919, however, made few changes and did not satisfy India's leaders. Although more Indians participated in provincial government than ever before, Indians still had little influence at the national level. Dissatisfaction resulted in a demonstration in 1919 at Amritsar. British troops fired on the crowds, killing over 300 people and wounding more than 1,000 others.

Following the Amritsar incident, a British-trained lawyer named Mohandas K. Gandhi (later also called Mahatma Gandhi) became the leader of the Indian National Congress. His policy of nonviolent resistance gained many supporters. Gandhi encouraged the boycott of foreign-made goods and the local production of textiles.

Gandhi's spiritual philosophy—called satyagraha, or truth consciousness—involved disobeying laws that he believed were discriminatory or immoral and accepting arrest for having broken the laws. His approach also included fasting as a means of protest. Since Gandhi's followers were unarmed and peaceful, the British were reluctant to attack them and usually only sent them to prison.

Demands for Self-Rule

Other groups joined the general cry for self-rule, and this trend further politicized the Indian population. The Sikhs, a people from the Punjab region, hoped their military support of British aims would win them special consideration. Untouchables (those who had the least-advantageous position within Indian society), socialists, and strict Hindus all aired their views. The Indian National Congress continued to attract many Indians and developed a Pan-Indian approach—that is, it sought to unite religious, language, and ethnic groups.

In contrast to Pan-Indian feelings, Mohammed Ali Jinnah, leader of the Muslim

League, demanded a separate Muslim voter roll and guaranteed representation for Muslims in any future independent Indian government. Jinnah's announcement showed how difficult it would be to devise a plan that would allow Hindu and Muslim communities to live in harmony after independence.

After negotiating with various Indian leaders, Britain passed a new Government of India Act in 1935. The plan tried both to satisfy the Indian desire for self-rule and to unite the states of the subcontinent into a single nation. Many Indian princes objected to the plan, because they felt that the new act weakened their power. Although princely resistance made it impossible to carry out the national part of the plan, the new legislation established fairly independent provincial governments. Members of the Indian National Congress dominated these regional councils.

The provincial governments held power from 1937 until the outbreak of World War II in 1939. During this two-year period, the idea of partitioning the subcontinent into separate Hindu and Muslim nations gained support among Muslims. They claimed that they were politically and culturally outnumbered by the Hindus and that their situation would only get worse in an independent India with a Hindu majority.

The Road to Independence

In 1939 Britain declared itself and its empire, including India, at war with Germany. Britain had not involved the Indian National Congress in making this decision, and the congress refused to cooperate with Great Britain during World War II. As an act of protest, congress leaders withdrew completely from the provincial government. The British response was to jail the congress leaders for the duration of the war.

The Muslim League, on the other hand, supported Britain fully during World War

Originally a member of the Indian National Congress, Mohammed Ali Jinnah became president of the Muslim League in 1913. By the 1930s he had come to view Partition—the division of India between Hindus and Muslims—as the only solution to problems of ethnic and religious inequality.

II. The league hoped to gain postwar recognition for the rights of the Muslim community. In 1940 Jinnah called for the establishment of a separate Muslim nation to be called Pakistan.

After the war ended in 1945, Britain's economy was weak and its army was ready to go home. The British could neither financially support their empire nor police their colonies. India's long-standing demand for self-rule further persuaded Britain that the time had come for Indian independence.

At first, the British tried to find common ground between the Indian National Congress and the Muslim League. But the split between the two groups was so great that agreement on a postindependence government proved impossible to reach. Partition, or division of India between Hindus and Muslims, appeared to be the only solution. Gandhi wanted to preserve Indian unity, but one of his longtime supporters in the congress, Jawaharlal Nehru, opted for Partition.

Partition and Independence

In June 1947 Britain announced a plan to establish two nations—India, with a Hindu majority, and Pakistan, with a Muslim majority—from its holdings on the subcontinent. The predominant religious group in a given region would determine to which nation each territory would belong. The plan allowed the princely states to join either nation or to remain independent.

The Congress party and the Muslim League agreed to the plan despite its complexities, and in August 1947 Britain formally acknowledged that India and Pakistan were independent. They became dominions within the British Commonwealth—that is, self-governing nations that acknowledged the British monarch as their ceremonial leader.

Migrations of refugees began immediately. Hindus living in Pakistan moved to India, and Muslims dwelling in India traveled to either West Pakistan or East Pakistan—the two wings of the new Muslim state. These movements—and Partition itself—caused Hindu-Muslim violence to erupt. Riots occurred in many large cities, and harassment of religious minorities in both countries forced many people who had never intended to move to flee to safety. During this period, Mahatma Gandhi urged understanding and nonviolence. A Hindu who believed Gandhi was too tolerant of Muslims assassinated him in 1948.

India Organizes

One of the first tasks of the new government was to unify India's separate states. The central government persuaded many princes to join the new nation by retain-

UPI/Bettmann Newsphotos

After Partition in 1947, hundreds of thousands of Muslims and Hindus crowded into and on top of trains that traveled through Amritsar—a city located on the border between the newly formed nations of India and Pakistan.

The design of India's flag was officially adopted in 1947. The chakra, an ancient Indian symbol for the powers of nature, lies on a central white stripe, which stands for peace. The orange and green bands signify courage and faith, respectively.

ing them as ceremonial heads of state and by paying them yearly pensions. The government used military force to compel Hyderabad—a large Hindu realm in central India ruled by a Muslim prince—to join the Indian union in 1948.

Jammu and Kashmir, a single Muslim state ruled by a Hindu prince, refused at first to join either nation. But Muslims from West Pakistan poured into the region and caused disturbances that the Hindu prince was unable to control. As a result, he decided to join the Indian union in 1948, and Indian troops restored order in the area. Since then, both India and Pakistan have claimed the territory. India bases its right to Jammu and Kashmir on the prince's 1948 decision. Pakistan, which refused to accept the prince's choice, continues to press for a statewide vote to determine the region's desires.

India's constitution, which went into effect in 1950, altered India's status from a dominion to a republic in the British Commonwealth. This change meant that India no longer recognized Britain's monarch as the ceremonial head of the Indian nation. Later reorganizations eliminated the power of the princes and created new states out of populations that spoke the same language.

National Development

After independence, India launched a plan for economic development under its first prime minister, Jawaharlal Nehru. He envisioned India with a mixed economy that would be able to both produce and distribute goods. Nehru wanted to use government money to improve irrigation techniques, to build hydroelectric power plants, and to broaden the transportation network. With public funds, he encouraged Indian manufacturers to produce items that India had previously imported. As a

35

result, India began to make its own heavy machinery and weapons.

In the 1950s and 1960s, along with Tito of Yugoslavia and Sukarno of Indonesia, Nehru brought together nations that sought political independence as well as participation in world events. These leaders formed the Nonaligned movement, which seeks to avoid being controlled by either of the world's superpowers—the United States or the Soviet Union.

In spite of successes at the international level, Nehru faced troubles along India's own borders. In December 1961 Indian forces invaded and eventually took over the small Portuguese territories of Goa, Daman, and Diu, which were located in coastal areas of southern India. In 1962 border wars with China developed in the Himalayas, resulting in Chinese troops overrunning Indian outposts. Western military aid did not alter the situation, which remained tense until China declared a cease-fire later that year.

Independent Picture Service

Jawaharlal Nehru was the son of Motilal Nehru, an early supporter of Gandhi. Educated in Great Britain as a lawyer, the younger Nehru returned to India in 1912 to practice his profession. He joined the Indian National Congress in 1919 and was imprisoned by the British several times between 1921 and 1945 for his political stance. During this period, he also was elected president of the congress. After India achieved independence in 1947, Nehru served as the nation's first prime minister until his death in 1964.

Courtesy of Jeannine Bayard and Kip Lilly

An Indian visitor prays at the eternal flame that honors Nehru and that lies within the grounds of his home in New Delhi.

Nehru placed modernization and industrial advancement high on his economic agenda. Here, machines separate cotton fibers at a factory in West Bengal.

Like her father, Jawaharlal Nehru, Indira Gandhi finished her education in Britain and was also imprisoned by the British for her political activities. In 1955 Gandhi won election to the executive board of the Congress party and began to carve her own niche in Indian politics.

The Rise of Indira Gandhi

After Nehru's death in 1964, border conflicts between India and Pakistan intensified. Nehru's successor, Lal Bahadur Shastri, eased the confrontation through a Soviet-sponsored cease-fire. A few hours after signing the document, Shastri died of a heart attack. After some political infighting, Nehru's daughter Indira Gandhi came to power as prime minister.

Following the 1967 elections, Gandhi's support weakened. The Congress party had only a small majority in the national legislature and no longer dominated half of the state legislatures. Coalitions and shifts of power became common in Indian national politics. In 1970 Gandhi asserted her leadership by backing a candidate for president different from the one put up by the Congress party. In response, the party expelled her, and she founded Congress (N)—her own political faction of the larger party. In the elections of 1971, Gandhi's new faction won a clear majority.

37

Events of the 1970s

A movement by the Bengali people in East Pakistan to establish a homeland called Bangladesh caused West Pakistan to station many troops in the eastern wing of the nation. Civil war broke out in 1971, and millions of East Pakistani refugees fled to India. Air raids into India from East Pakistan provoked an invasion by Indian troops, who quickly defeated the forces of Pakistan. Soon afterward, East Pakistan declared itself the independent Republic of Bangladesh. In April 1974 India, Pakistan, and Bangladesh signed an agreement guaranteeing the return of prisoners of war and the exchange of occupied territories.

Although Gandhi held power within Congress (N), the smaller parties disliked her aggressive style of leadership and her political direction. By mid-1975 all of the opposition parties had combined to pass a no-confidence measure in the legislature against Gandhi. (Under the constitution, such a motion means that government leaders must resign from office.) In addition, India's highest court declared Gandhi guilty of election violations in 1971 and barred her from Parliament for six years. Gandhi's response was to declare a state of emergency, which made it legal for her to suspend the constitution and to jail those opposed to her policies.

Gandhi's harsh measures—especially a birth control scheme to sterilize Indian males who had fathered two or more children—met with strong resistance. Her imprisonment of respected political figures, such as Morarji Desai, caused her to lose popularity on a large scale. Resentment also arose against her son Sanjay, who put many of the emergency measures into effect. Although the Indian people had never elected him to political office, Sanjay was one of the most powerful figures in India.

In 1977 the prime minister dissolved the legislature and called national elections, in which she and her party were badly

Independent Picture Service

Head of the Janata party, Morarji Desai became India's prime minister in 1977. One of his first acts was to end the state of emergency declared by Indira Gandhi in 1971.

defeated. Morarji Desai became prime minister as the head of the new Janata party—an alliance of four anti-Gandhi groups.

The Desai coalition tried to distribute power more equally throughout the government, but the new leadership suffered from political infighting. Street violence slowed the new government's efforts to revive public freedoms that the Gandhis had limited. The coalition fell apart in December 1979, and competition among those who wanted to succeed Desai further weakened the Janata party.

The Modern Era

Elections in 1980 brought Indira Gandhi back to power as prime minister. The legal actions against Gandhi and her son Sanjay were dropped. Sanjay, who was being prepared to succeed his mother, died in a plane crash in 1980. Thereafter, Indira Gandhi's hopes for continuing her policies came to rest on her other son, Rajiv.

During the next few years, internal conflicts arose as protests in Assam and Punjab ended in violence. One such confrontation involved an assault on the Golden Temple at Amritsar, a revered shrine of people who follow the Sikh religion. Partly as a result of that attack, two of the prime minister's Sikh bodyguards assassinated her in October 1984, and Rajiv Gandhi became the premier. General elections soon followed, and the new prime minister won the largest majority of any political leader in Indian history.

Situated in the center of Amritsar, the Golden Temple is the most sacred site for Sikh believers. In 1984 and 1986 Sikh extremists occupied the temple during violent uprisings in Punjab, and the site has become a flash point for Hindu-Sikh confrontations.

Wearing a traditional silver bracelet and kirpan, or dagger, a Sikh guard patrols the Golden Temple at Amritsar—the Sikh holy city in Punjab.

In an attempt to solve some of India's long-standing problems, Gandhi signed a peace accord in Punjab with the region's leaders. By 1986, however, Punjab had disintegrated nearly into civil war as Sikh nationalists and government troops clashed. In addition, several members of Gandhi's inner circle were involved in a number of scandals. As a result, Gandhi's popular support has declined, and new elections scheduled in 1989 threaten his power within the legislature.

Continuing Challenges

India's major internal problem in the late 1980s remains Punjab, where Sikhs have

Although India has made much progress in improving its economy, many people – such as these who live in a Calcutta slum – face economic hardships.

Photo by Josh Kohnstamm

long agitated for greater independence within the Indian union. In recent years the agitation has become increasingly violent, with Sikh terrorists attacking Hindu villages in Punjab. In response, anti-Sikh riots have occurred in New Delhi. The situation presents a challenge to India's leaders, because many other separatist groups—such as those in Assam—are waiting to see what happens in Punjab.

In addition, India has become involved in Sri Lanka's civil war by establishing a peacekeeping army on the island to try to ease the tensions between the minority Sri Lankan Tamil and the majority Sinhalese.

Hundreds of Indian soldiers have been killed in this ongoing conflict. India has also begun to buy and export military equipment in large quantities.

Despite these signs of tension, India has maintained its nonaligned stance toward the United States and the Soviet Union. Government policies have also encouraged economic progress, particularly in the production of grain, electronic equipment, weaponry, and machines. Nevertheless, almost 40 percent of India's population live below the official poverty line, and government policies have yet to improve basic conditions in many regions.

Government

Under the constitution adopted in 1950, India is a parliamentary republic. An electoral college consisting of members of Parliament chooses a president, whose duties are essentially ceremonial, every five years. Real power is in the hands of the prime minister, who is elected by Parliament. The prime minister may dissolve Parliament and call for new elections before the end of the allotted five-year term.

Legislative power rests with a two-house Parliament that consists of an upper house, called the Rajya Sabha (Council of States), and a lower house, named the Lok Sabha (House of the People). The state legislatures elect all members of the upper house, except for 12 whom the president appoints. Members of the lower house are directly elected, with the exception of 10 delegates who are named by the president.

The central and state governments handle activities within India's judicial system, which has its roots in British law. The highest Indian tribunal is the supreme court, whose members are appointed to lifelong terms by the president. High, district, and magistrate courts complete the judicial structure.

In 1989 India was made up of 22 states, including Jammu and Kashmir, and 9 union territories. State and territorial governments are miniatures of the central government. They have extensive authority over local affairs and are responsible for education, health, and other services at the regional level.

On the local level, community governmental functions belong to village councils, or panchayats. Villagers elect the members of the panchayats, which serve as intermediaries between villages and state governments.

Architects designed Parliament House – where India's legislature meets – to stand at one end of an imaginary straight line that runs through the modern city of New Delhi to the Jami Masjid in old Delhi. The modern structure represents India's new direction, and the mosque is a reminder of the nation's long history.

A tiny portion of India's more than 800 million people crowd a street in Madurai, a city in the southern state of Tamil Nadu.

3) The People

After China, India has the largest population of any country in the world. With 835 million inhabitants, India is home to 6 percent of the world's population, although it occupies only 2 percent of the world's land. To compound the problem of high population density, the number of people in India is predicted to double in 32 years. One of the few factors that keeps the population figure from rising more rapidly is India's high rate of infant mortality. Nearly 100 of every 1,000 Indian babies die before they reach the age of five.

Arid regions of western India are sparsely populated, while the southern tip, the Coromandel Coast, and the states of West Bengal, Bihar, and Uttar Pradesh are crowded. India's overall density per square mile is over 500 people, but in Calcutta the ratio averages 79,000 people per square mile of urban territory. Despite a number of large cities, about 75 percent of the population live in rural communities of fewer than 5,000 people.

India's Ethnic Diversity

Various ethnic groups and cultural strains make up India's widely diverse population. Most of India's people have mixed Caucasian, Asian, and African ethnic roots. People with Dravidian backgrounds orig-

Courtesy of Nathan Rabe

During the dry season, a villager near the holy city of Allahabad in Uttar Pradesh carries a pan on his head as he walks along a dusty road.

inally resided in northern India about 4,000 years ago, during the time of the Indus civilization. As a result of invasion, the Dravidians moved south, where today their descendants form the majority ethnic group on the peninsula.

The invaders of the north were Aryans from central Asia, and their descendants in the region came to be called Indo-Aryans or Indo-Europeans. Islamic peoples arrived via Afghanistan and Iran in about A.D. 1000. They settled in the northeast, and their descendants still live in West Bengal, Bihar, and Uttar Pradesh. The Himalayan region attracted central Asians from more remote regions, and the mountains prevented their culture from blending completely with those of other peoples.

The Caste System

India's caste system still controls the lifestyles of its people. Birth determines one's social level, and members of the wealthiest and most prestigious group are called Brahmans, who make up the priestly caste. In descending order of importance are the Kshatriyas, the caste from which warriors and rulers come; the Vaisyas, who are merchants and artisans; and the Sudras, who work as servants and manual laborers.

The panchamas, or outcasts, belong to no caste and, as a result, are considered outside of the traditional social and economic framework. Also known as untouchables, they make up about one-fifth of India's entire population. Mahatma Gandhi, who fought to end discrimination against them, coined a new term for them —Harijans, meaning "people of God."

Complex rules govern contact between people of different castes at all levels of Indian society. People infrequently marry

A newly married couple wear necklaces of colorful flowers after their wedding ceremony in the state of Gujarat in western India.

Courtesy of Nathan Rabe

someone from outside their caste, and members of high castes will only eat meals prepared by high-caste cooks. On the other hand, the same cook could feed people of a lower caste. Caste determines the profession one follows and the people with whom one associates.

Although the new Indian constitution prohibits discrimination based on these social barriers, the system continues to flourish. The caste system has deep historical roots, supports an economic structure, and helps Indians to define who they are. As a result, caste consciousness is unlikely to disappear until an equally complete social system evolves.

Languages and Literature

Hindi is the official language of the Republic of India, but many citizens know it only as a second language. Within schools, classes are taught in the language of the region, and at the university level English is commonly used.

About 1,600 languages are spoken in India. This huge number reveals the country's cultural diversity. The languages include Bengali, Bihari, Hindi, Panjabi, Urdu, Marathi, Rajasthani, Gujarati, Oriya, Kashmiri, Assamese, and Pahari—all of which belong to the Indo-European family of languages. Roughly 75 percent of the Indian population speak an Indo-European tongue. Tamil, Kannada, Telugu, and Malayalam are members of the Dravidian family of languages, which about 25 percent of Indians use as their primary form of speech.

The subcultures of India not only differ in spoken languages but also in the alphabets they use to write each language. Un-

Within the major caste group are many subgroups, each of which has a specific task. These men are members of India's farming caste.

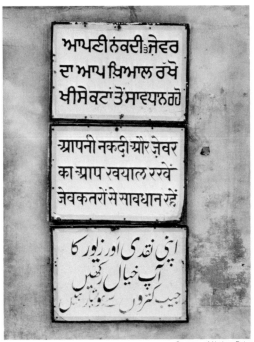

A sign in Panjabi, Hindi, and Urdu warns against pickpockets.

Writing in the Bengali language, Rabindranath Tagore became one of India's most famous poets and often used images of the Bengal countryside in his verse.

like English, French, and Italian, which all employ the same letters in different combinations, many of India's languages—such as Bengali, Hindi, and Marathi—use their own versions of the Nagari or Sanskritic alphabet.

Indian literature has an ancient tradition and has been influenced primarily by religion. The four Vedas, or sacred books of Hinduism, were written in Sanskrit in about 1500 B.C. and contain Hindu law and philosophy. Indians still read the four Vedas for the ideals they express and for the beauty of their language. More famous in the Western world are India's folk epics, such as the *Bhagavad-Gita* (Song of the Blessed Krishna). Rabindranath Tagore, who won the Nobel prize for literature in 1913, is among the most widely read of India's twentieth-century writers.

Education

Since independence, India has tried to improve the nation's educational system. The country's literacy rate is still fairly low—57 percent for men and 29 percent for women —although these figures have improved since 1950. The government has devoted increasing amounts of its annual budget to build schools, to train teachers, and to supply educational materials.

India's schools are under the direct authority of the states, but the national government provides financial help and centralized planning. The free educational system includes eight years of elementary classes and three of secondary schooling.

About 90 percent of the children aged 6 to 14 attend classes, but only 20 percent of older students are enrolled at the secondary level. Fewer children go to school in rural areas, where not as many schools exist and where poor economic conditions sometimes require children to work. Nevertheless, India's schools are generally overcrowded.

India has over 4,000 colleges and more than 100 universities. Only 3 percent of

Students listen to their teacher in an outdoor classroom in Bihar state.

university-aged people attend institutions of higher learning. Among the main schools are Agra University, the University of Bombay, and the University of Calcutta.

Health

Despite government efforts to improve living conditions, Indians continue to suffer from poor health. Substandard diets, un- safe water, and inadequate medical facilities have increased the nation's health risks.

In 1989 life expectancy was 58 years (up from 32 in 1950), and about half of the entire population had access to safe drinking water. Government programs to wipe out disease have resulted in fewer cases of malaria, cholera, smallpox, and tuberculosis. A large segment of the population continues

Using pictures, a health-care worker passes on nutrition and birth control advice to a group of Indian women.

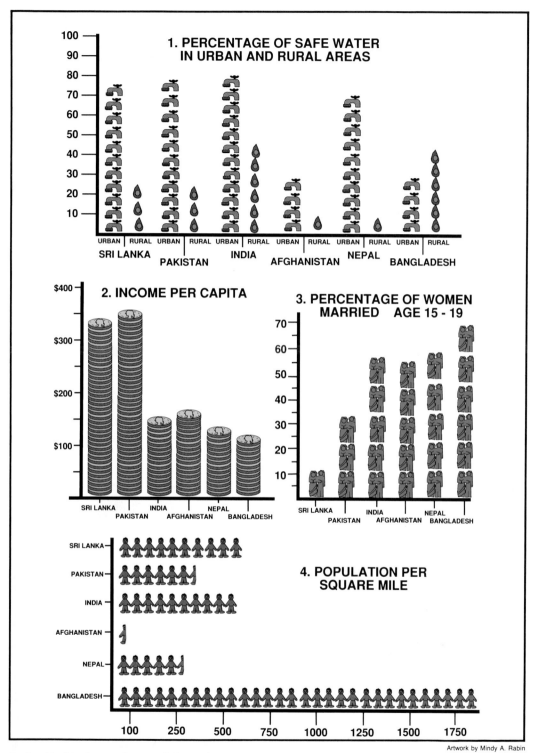

1. PERCENTAGE OF SAFE WATER IN URBAN AND RURAL AREAS

URBAN	RURAL	URBAN	RURAL	URBAN	RURAL
SRI LANKA		PAKISTAN		INDIA	

URBAN	RURAL	URBAN	RURAL	URBAN	RURAL
AFGHANISTAN		NEPAL		BANGLADESH	

2. INCOME PER CAPITA

SRI LANKA
PAKISTAN
INDIA
AFGHANISTAN
NEPAL
BANGLADESH

3. PERCENTAGE OF WOMEN MARRIED AGE 15 - 19

SRI LANKA
PAKISTAN
INDIA
AFGHANISTAN
NEPAL
BANGLADESH

4. POPULATION PER SQUARE MILE

SRI LANKA
PAKISTAN
INDIA
AFGHANISTAN
NEPAL
BANGLADESH

100 250 500 750 1000 1250 1500 1750

Artwork by Mindy A. Rabin

Depicted in this chart are factors relating to the standard of living in six countries in southern Asia. (Information taken from "1987 World Population Data Sheet," "The World's Women: A Profile," and "Children of the World" compiled by the Population Reference Bureau, Washington, D.C.)

to suffer from malnutrition. Health clinics exist throughout the republic, but rural people have trouble reaching them. Government-sponsored health-care services have encouraged Indians to have fewer children, yet only one-third of Indian women of child-bearing age use birth control.

The Arts

Traditional Indian art occurs in a variety of forms. Rock-hewn caves, as well as huge above-ground temples, are adorned with thousands of sculpted images, making Hindu architecture lavish and rich. In contrast, the Taj Mahal, a fine example of Islamic architecture, has a simpler approach. Built of white marble and ornamented with exquisite mosaics of precious stone, it is one of the world's most beautiful buildings.

Delicate Indian miniature paintings present a mass of small details, and larger artworks sometimes feature sensual human figures and may portray a Buddhist story.

Courtesy of Clarice Wilson

In Chandigarh, Punjab, unique statues—made in the 1970s of discarded materials—are a feature of the city's Rock Garden.

Historically, miniatures depicted life within the upper levels of Indian society. The golden age of this style of artwork was between the sixteenth and eighteenth centuries.

Courtesy of Nathan Rabe

The ornate and relaxed style of Hindu sculpture is evident in a temple carving from Madurai.

Independent Picture Service

Underscoring the delicate skill of the sculptor is the marble ceiling of the Tejpal Temple. This holy Jain site is located at Dilwara in the hills of Rajasthan.

48

A miniature painting from about 1630 depicts a scene from a *ragmala* – a set of poems that describes the 36 modes, or melodic patterns, used in Indian music.

Courtesy of Museum of Fine Arts, Boston

Independent Picture Service

Dance is one of the most widely cultivated art forms in India. The gestures of the hands, the positions of the neck, and the motions of the eyes are the most striking features of Indian dances. Some dances, such as bharata natya in Tamil Nadu, are very old. Kathakali dancers wear heavy makeup to dramatize ancient characters, and Manipuri performers sway gracefully in the wide skirts that are part of their traditional costumes.

India's film industry is the second largest in the world, and the nation's films are exported to nearly 100 foreign countries. Several movies have won prizes at international film festivals. The Film and

Wearing the traditional wide-skirted costume, a Manipuri performer does one of the ras dances, which portray the legend of the Hindu god Krishna and his wife Radha.

49

A bharata natya dancer learns to position her hands and neck with precise artistry.

A larger-than-life poster announces a motion picture in Madras—India's biggest movie center after the city of Bombay.

Television Institute, created in 1961, provides training in all aspects of filmmaking. Many films, including those of Satyajit Ray, discuss the way that changes in Indian society—from colonialism to independence, for example—affect everyday Indian life.

Religion

More than 80 percent of India's population follow the Hindu religion. Although Hindus have a core of common beliefs, room exists in Hinduism for varying—even contradictory—ideas.

Hindu pilgrims to the sacred Ganges River make religious offerings, which they position on floating leaves and then push across the waterway.

HINDUISM

Foremost among the tenets of Hinduism is faith in the existence of the Brahman, or supreme soul of the universe. Of nearly equal importance is the belief that all souls eventually return to and merge with the Brahman. This return takes place, however, only after the individual has lived through a series of earthly lives. Karma is the name that Hindus give to this individ-

Built in 1938, the modern Laxmi Narayan Temple in New Delhi is dedicated to the Hindu god Vishnu and his wife Laxmi, the goddess of wealth.

ual destiny. They think of the experience of living as preparation for a higher existence that begins only after they are released from the long cycle of birth, death, and rebirth.

Caste determines a person's social role and responsibilities, collectively called dharma. The fulfillment of one's dharma is considered the job of every Hindu. In addition to the notions of the Brahman, karma, and dharma, there is a fourth major concept of Hinduism called maya. This belief suggests that the world and its people are illusions and that only the Brahman is real.

ISLAM AND CHRISTIANITY

Of India's other religions, Islam is the largest and is supported by about 10 percent of the population. Two main religious sects—Shiism and Sunnism—exist in Islam. Most Muslim villages in India are made up of people from one sect or the other. Because the number of Hindu converts to Islam is large, many Hindu customs and traditions survive in India's Muslim communities.

Faithful Muslims fulfill several obligations, which include daily prayer, fasting, charitable donations, and pilgrimage. In large villages, mosques (Muslim places of prayer) stand alongside Hindu temples. Conflicts between Hindus and Muslims erupt frequently, but less often because of religious issues than because of differences in political goals.

Christianity, which 2 percent of India's population follow, is the oldest imported religion in the country. Part of the Christian community is made up of descendants of the Nestorians, an unorthodox Christian sect that arose in the first few centuries of the Christian era. Other Indian Christians are descendants of people whom Western missionaries converted during the colonial period.

In the courtyard of old Delhi's Jami Masjid, Muslims bow toward the Saudi Arabian holy city of Mecca to say their prayers.

SIKHISM, JAINISM, AND BUDDHISM

Thirteen million Sikhs and three million Jains—collectively about 2 percent of the population—follow religions that are native to India. Both systems arose as reform sects of Hinduism. Sikhism was founded in the late fifteenth century to end the differences between Hindus and Muslims through a new religion that combined elements of both Hinduism and Islam. One of the original aims of the religion was to abolish the Hindu caste system. The Sikh community has evolved into an aggressive group and has forced the government to establish a separate Sikh state called Haryana.

A nearly complete thirteenth-century Jain temple has survived in the hills of Rajasthan and is dedicated to Neminath, the twenty-second Tirthankara, or Jain prophet.

Food and Clothing

Grains, such as wheat, barley, and rice, are an important part of the diet of most Indians. Also featured are vegetables that come from seed pods, such as beans and peas. Curry—a blend of strong spices—gives its name to one of India's most famous dishes. Generally, curries consist of eggs, vegetables, meat, or fish that are cooked in a highly seasoned sauce.

The method of making bread differs between northern and southern India. In the north, chapati are made from dough that has been rolled flat and cooked on a griddle. Southern Indians soak rice or seeds to make a paste, which they drop as round balls into boiling oil to form a hollow bread called *roti*.

Courtesy of Jeannine Bayard and Kip Lilly

Followers of the Buddhist religion in Darjeeling carry banners in celebration of the birth, death, and enlightenment of Gautama Buddha—the founder of the faith.

Mahavira (meaning the Great Hero) founded Jainism in the sixth century B.C. and taught that all life was sacred. Devout Jains neither gamble nor eat meat. They usually abstain from sexual activity and have few belongings. The strict lifestyle of Jains receives much respect in India.

An Indian prince, Siddhartha Gautama (later called Gautama Buddha—a title meaning "enlightened one"), established Buddhism in India in the sixth century B.C. Today less than 1 percent of Indians practices the Buddhist faith. Gautama Buddha's teaching stressed moral duties and good behavior and arose as a reaction against the complex rituals of Hinduism. Emperor Asoka adopted Buddhism in the third century B.C. and made it the official religion of the Maurya dynasty. Although the faith lost favor in India after Asoka's death, it spread to China, Korea, Southeast Asia, and Japan.

Courtesy of Nathan Rabe

To bring the stongest flavor to Indian food, most cooks in India freshly grind their spices every day.

India's generally hot climate causes people to adopt light clothing in most areas of the country. Men often wrap cloths around themselves to form loose trousers, or they wear finished trousers that are loose at the waist and tightly fitted between the knee and ankle. Saris— long pieces of fabric draped like dresses— are very popular among Indian women. The brightly dyed cloth is usually long enough to use part of it as a veil or head covering. The fabric is often woven from locally produced cotton. In urban areas Western-style clothing is also common.

Courtesy of FAO

In Gujarat, an Indian woman prepares chapati—flat wheat bread—on an improved, smokeless stove.

Photo by Josh Kohnstamm

Wearing brightly colored saris— draped cloths that are a traditional style of dress in India—these women shop for the day's food.

Laborers painstakingly plant individual rice cuttings by hand in a flooded paddy on India's eastern coast.

4) The Economy

India has a strong and varied economic base, yet its growing population continues to keep it within the ranks of the world's poorest nations. A series of five-year plans governs the country's economic progress and focuses government funds on specific goals.

Several of these five-year plans have aimed to increase India's manufacturing output, and business districts in major Indian cities reveal the great progress India has made in industry and technology. Products fashioned in India, with Indian components and expertise, now range from refrigerators to video recorders.

The central government controls most major industries, and it manages the flow of raw materials and sets production guidelines. In the 1980s the Indian government loosened its grip on the economy and allowed producers to participate more freely in foreign markets. India is also a regional economic power and exports technology, skilled labor, and finished goods throughout the Middle East, Asia, Africa, and Europe.

Although industry has progressed, the economy is still primarily agricultural. As a result, it is vulnerable to drought and flood, and most of India's population still exists on the subsistence level—that is, farmers produce only enough crops to meet the needs of their families.

Agriculture

Farming employs about 70 percent of India's working population, and agriculture provides roughly 40 percent of the nation's yearly income. Approximately half of India's land is under cultivation.

Previous five-year plans have focused on improving the agricultural sector. As a result, better farming methods, higher-quality seeds, and good fertilizers have increased food production. These efforts have brought India closer to producing all of its own food, although droughts and floods—the most recent setbacks were in 1987—have occasionally slowed progress.

Some farmers practice a nomadic style of agriculture, in which they clear a section of forest, plant crops, and move on after a few years when the soil has become less fertile. Family members tend most plots, which are usually less than five acres and which the farmers plant twice each year. One sowing occurs after the rains begin in the floodplains, where rice, cotton, and jute thrive. Another planting season begins when the rains are over and involves crops like wheat, barley, and linseed. Commercial farming—for export crops such as tea, coffee, or rubber—often takes place on large plantations using hired labor.

CROPS AND LIVESTOCK

Rice, a common food in the Indian diet, is the most important and the most widespread crop. Indian farmers cultivate over 4,000 kinds of rice, generally in delta regions along the east coast. In the mid-1980s workers harvested more than 80

A boy in the state of Orissa works in a flourishing rice field surrounded by stalks of the fast-growing crop.

Modern machinery is used to harvest much of India's wheat crop.

Tea plants cover the Nilgiri Hills in southern India.

million tons of rice annually, and India became the largest producer of the grain after China.

Wheat, a staple in northern India, is the nation's second major food crop. Because wheat can thrive in drier conditions than rice can, it grows in more places throughout the country. Madhya Pradesh, Uttar Pradesh, and Punjab are among the main wheat-producing states. Although yields of wheat doubled between 1960 and 1980, India must still import large amounts of the grain each year to keep up with domestic demand.

Tea, jute, cotton, tobacco, coffee, and sugar are the chief commercial crops. Tea, India's major export crop, grows mostly on large plantations. Important during the colonial period, the tea harvest has continued to increase both in quantity and export value since independence.

India's vast textile industry is based on the nation's cotton crop, which reached 1.4 million tons in the mid-1980s. Commercial mills in India used most of that amount to weave cloth. India is the world's second largest cultivator of jute (a fibrous plant used in making burlap and twine) and

57

Courtesy of Air-India Library

Most of India's cattle—such as these tough zebu cows—are raised for farm labor, not for their meat.

produced over one million tons of the fiber in the mid-1980s.

Tobacco and coffee rank second and third among India's crops that bring in large amounts of foreign revenue. Since the early 1980s India has emerged as a major sugarcane grower, ranking third in the world among producers of raw sugar.

Hinduism discourages the eating of beef and regards cows as sacred symbols of purity. As a result, the slaughter of cattle is relatively rare. The chief beasts of burden are cattle and camels. Most Indians use them for milking and as labor animals. Poultry and sheep are the main sources of meat, although few Indians can afford meat as part of their daily diets.

OPIUM AND CANNABIS

India also harvests the largest legally grown crop of opium poppies in the world. The plants are the raw material for some legal drugs, such as morphine, and are used to make the illegal substances opium and heroin. In recent times, more illegally grown opium poppies, as well as shipments from nearby opium-producing nations, have remained in India to satisfy a growing local drug demand. By 1984 heroin had become India's second most abused drug, after cannabis (the source of hashish and marijuana). Cannabis plants grow well in India and are refined to supply most of the demands of the domestic hashish market.

Industry and Mining

The Indian government regards the rapid expansion of industry as a crucial factor in the country's future prosperity. Indeed, the government's next five-year plan will devote more funds to industry than to agriculture. Current efforts concentrate on manufacturing capital goods—machines and other products that are used in other industries. As a result, the production of iron, steel, heavy machinery, and tools has increased in recent decades. By 1978 machinery and transportation equipment surpassed in value India's longtime leading exports—tea and jute.

Other important products include burlap bags, textiles, cement, matches, paper, leather goods, and chemicals. Indian factories make sugar and tea, refine oil, and process cashew nuts. India is also the world's largest supplier of cut diamonds, which are imported in their uncut form from South Africa. Small-scale industries that contribute to India's economy produce works of brass, marble, ivory, wood, silk, and cotton.

Although India is the world's seventh largest steel-producing country, it is unable to manufacture enough steel for its own requirements. The main raw materials

After the discovery of offshore oil, India built several drilling platforms—such as this one near Bombay—in the waters surrounding the subcontinent.

for making steel—coal and iron ore—are abundant in India. The nation's most fully exploited coal and iron deposits are close to Jamshedpur in northeastern India. Mining complexes also extract bauxite (the raw material for aluminum), manganese, mica (a thin, transparent metal), copper, and chromite.

In the late 1970s India suffered economically because of the high price of petroleum. Recently, however, large natural gas and oil reserves have been discovered both within India and off its shores, and these deposits have begun to satisfy India's petroleum needs.

Forestry and Fishing

Much of India's previously forested areas now support only scrub vegetation, and deforestation has reduced the percentage

India's industrial sector has seen great advancement in recent decades, and the nation now produces most of its own heavy machinery and cables.

In a rural area of India, villagers chop up a recent harvest of wood for use as fuel.

Fishermen in the state of Kerala throw out their nets to gather the day's catch in one of the region's coastal lagoons.

of wooded land to about one-fifth of the nation's total territory. Stands of hardwoods, including sal and teak, are located in areas with heavy rainfall and high altitudes, such as the states of Madhya Pradesh, Orissa, Maharashtra, and Andhra Pradesh. The sale of wood by-products—pulp, fibers, oils, and resins, for example—contributes to the income from forestry.

With its long coastlines and many inland streams, India has great potential as a fishing nation. About one-third of the country's fishing zone—which extends for over 200 miles into the ocean—is used for fishing. Of freshwater fish, Indian fishermen value catfish and carp. Saltwater catches include mackerel, sardines, Bombay ducks, herring, anchovies, tuna, and shrimp.

Fishermen market most of their hauls as fresh fish, and the remainder appear in dried form. The government has contributed funds to promote the processing of frozen fish. As a result, frozen shrimp have become India's most valuable seafood export, the majority of which went to Japan in the 1980s.

Energy and Transportation

Although wood is the main fuel in areas where electricity is scarce, urban regions receive power from a variety of energy sources. India's industrial sector uses most of the country's coal to power its factories. Oil and natural gas provide about one-third of the nation's energy, but, despite petroleum deposits within India, the nation still imports some oil. Nuclear-powered reactors have been built in Bombay and Madras and in the states of Rajasthan and Uttar Pradesh. But costs to construct such plants are high, and India currently gets only 1 percent of its electricity from nuclear power.

India's large river network could provide large amounts of hydroelectricity. Most of the potential sites, however, lie in the

The Krishnarajasagar Dam harnesses the power of the Cauvery River, which flows through the states of Karnataka and Tamil Nadu.

61

A remnant of the era of the British Empire in India is Bombay's Victoria Terminus railway station—often referred to among the city's residents simply as VT.

Passengers crowd the doors, windows, and roofs of India's trains as still others wait in line to find places in the packed railway cars.

Himalayas, where access is difficult and where few urban centers exist. Seasonal water flow, which is dependent on monsoon rains, has also affected the development of hydropower plants. As a result, only 5 percent of the nation's water resources are being exploited.

India has the fourth largest railway system in the world, and the largest one in Asia. The government-owned network has about 37,500 miles of track and carries more than 3.7 billion passengers each year. India's railways employ over one million workers, and the nation's industrial sector manufactures the network's cars and engines. About 5,000 miles of navigable inland waterways supplement the railway system, and one million miles of roads crisscross the subcontinent.

Air India and Indian Airlines, both government-owned, connect major cities within India and link the nation to over 20 countries on five continents. Four international airports and many smaller airfields operate throughout the country. Cargo and passenger ships dock at India's main port cities—Calcutta, Bombay, Madras, Vishakhapatnam, and Goa.

The Future

In 1987 Indians celebrated 40 years of independence—an achievement that in 1947 many people believed would never occur. India has a healthy economy, as well as respect within the international community, and it has made steady progress against the long-standing challenges of poverty and illiteracy.

Despite signs of growth and improvement, however, political discontent and religious and ethnic violence still disturb the nation. India's relations with its neighbors—especially Pakistan and China—remain cool on almost every border and add to tension in the region. Smaller nations resent India's interference in their internal matters, while India regards itself as the dominant power of the region.

Courtesy of India Tourism Development Corporation, Ltd.
In rural areas, boats are a common form of transport.

Although uncertainties exist in India's future, young Indians have become active in the nation's political and economic arenas. The country's progress or decline during the coming decades rests with this new generation.

Courtesy of Embassy of India
Prime Minister Rajiv Gandhi is the fourth generation of political activists in his family, beginning with his great-grandfather Motilal Nehru.

Index